ONESINGLELADY:
A Guide to Single Christian Living

Introduction

Being a single Christian woman living in a secular world is difficult if you are relying on your own strength. There are so many temptations from the outside world to confirm to its ways, and they are strong. Not only are there temptations from outside, we are tempted by our hearts, which are desperately wicked as well. Considering this, there is nothing we can do on our own to navigate the rocky waters of the sea of temptations. Only through the strength of God and the Holy Spirit living on the inside of us are we able to ward off the thoughts that tempt and plague us.

Everything in this book is related to a method to combat the temptations that arise in the life of a single Christian woman. Whether it be temptation to be dissatisfied with life because of loneliness or envy, or seeking harmful relationships that are not healthy with those who we are not equally yoked. This book also talks about getting closer to the Lord, forming healthy friendships, and more! This information is meant for encouragement and comes from a combination of personal experience, and the words of wise women who have come before me and shared their lives with me. Enjoy!

Foreword

As a single Christian woman dating in today's society, I am excited about this devotional guide.

There are a lot of do's and don't's that stem from our mothers, grandmothers, and father figures that are great advice. However, the greatest advice comes from the Word.

Taking a daily approach as Ashley outlines in this guide helps us to strategically walk in our singleness as Christian women. Knowing what the Bible says and being obedient not only pleases God, but it reduces the heartache associated with failed relationships simply because God is at the forefront of our decision making process. This guide will force us to face the most important question in many situations, if not all: is this pleasing to God? The answer will either confirm that we're progressing in the right direction or it serves as a redirect to get us back on the right path when it comes to being a virtuous woman. So, I invite you to take this journey, fully embrace it, and put the words into action until God sends your Boaz!

Jaemellah Kemp
Jaemellah Kemp
Consultant, Philanthropist, and Nonprofit Entrepreneur

Day 1

Being A Little Fish in a Big Sea of Marrieds and Couples

When you are single, a lot of times, it feels like *everybody you meet* is getting together. And when you walk down the street, you seem to only notice the people holding hands or the couples sharing a good laugh at coffee tables. But is that really the right perspective to have? Moreover, is that even a way of looking at the world that is close to reality? No!

The reality is there are hundreds of people walking down that same street who are single, just like you. And some of them are perfectly content with this state of singleness. What's their trick? Well I am here to tell you, it is no magic trick there is no divine moment of truth where your whole life changes. It is just a simple decision to live your life for God and only God and desire to do what He wants you to do. Does this sound it is challenging? Nothing in this life comes easy because of sin. But the first step is making the commitment.

It is easier for us single women to be concerned with the desires of God. But I think we often fool ourselves into thinking it is going to be difficult because we are unwilling to rely on the Lord for strength. This is something that I

1 Corinthians 7:34 tells us this in a nutshell: [34]and his interests are divided. And the unmarried or betrothed woman is anxious about the things of the Lord, how to be holy in body and spirit. But the married woman is anxious about

am learning right along with you ladies! So be encouraged, you are not alone, and reach out to older women in your lives who can guide you in this walk and answer questions that you have. Older women have paved the way, blazed trails, and are a lot more knowledgeable than even your best girl friend or the latest magazine article. Yes, I said it.

Older women in your churches and other older Christian women in your life have more knowledge in their databases than Essence and Vogue! Seek out these women of God who have stored up knowledge in their hearts and minds, and start to tap into that knowledge. You will find your life enriched tremendously because of this. It takes faith and prayer to find the right person to approach about talking about being single and your struggles, but do believe me, it is worth your while.   This book is your guide to different ideas or concepts that are essential to surviving and thriving in this world as a young single Christian lady.

Day 2

Having Faith When It Seems You Will Never Find "The One"

I have had enough of being single, you might say. I want someone to take me out to chick flicks because I like them and because he wants to do whatever I want to do! I want someone to have long conversations on the phone with me, to play "You hang up, no you hang up," until one of us falls asleep or accidentally hits the button! God knows the desires of your heart. Notice the Scripture in the box below does not say – If God gives me the desires of my heart, I will then delight myself in Him.

> Psalm 37:4 says, "If you delight yourself in the Lord, he will give you the desires of your heart."

It is a process which first starts with a focus and a zeroing in on God. You need to start delighting yourself in Him NOW!

What does delighting yourself in Him look like to you? And do you believe that you are single because that is what God has for you, or do you just feel unwanted? In my experience, it has been told to me that "God wants you to be single right now, and that is why you are." I'm sure that you have had that same experience. It's true! If you are single right now, you are right where God wants you to be. Pursue delighting Him and He will make straight your paths and show you the way to achieve your dreams!

Day 3

Making the Choice

When we fall, whether it be backsliding or just sinning against another person, oftentimes we do not want to take the step to correct the wrong. It might be painful, or embarrassing. Or both. It might force us to face secret desires in our hearts that we have been nurturing that are not of God. Or it may lead us to separate ourselves from people who we enjoy being around. No matter what the circumstance, if we are to call ourselves Christians, we must be above reproach. We should attack our sins, through prayer and constantly keeping watch over our lips and actions.

In Jeremiah, the Israelites are going through a similar situation. They have been backsliding, and here is what the Lord says to them:

Look at what the Lord says He will do for the Israelites. He will bring them, "to Zion," and "give. . .shepherds after my own heart, who will feed. . . with knowledge and

Jeremiah 3:13-15

13 Only acknowledge your guilt, that you rebelled against the LORD your God and scattered your favors among foreigners under every green tree, and that you have not obeyed my voice, declares the LORD. 14 Return, O faithless children, declares the LORD;

understanding." We too are the Lord's people. He will bring us to Zion if we return to Him.

But first we must make that choice to return to Him. We must get back up. We should return to our sister and ask for forgiveness, attempt to reconcile with our mother who we haven't spoken to now for weeks. We need to return to church and really listen to the message, to see what God wants us to hear about Him. And in situations where we have sinned against another person, and/or feel we have been sinned against, we need to remember one thing. We are not apologizing or forgiving so that they will change, but so that we will grow.

As far as harboring desires that are not of God, we need to turn those desires over to the Lord and return to Him, walk alongside of Him again and pray daily over those desires. We need to make a conscious effort not to think on those things, but also not to try to fight the battle on our own. Because on our own strength, we are weak, but with God's strength and love flowing through us, we are strong. That does not mean we will stop struggling, or that we will not fall again. However, we are making a choice to honor God, and that is what He ultimately cares about.

Day 4

Expecting Respect

We are daughters of God, fearfully and wonderfully made. Do not let anyone treat you as if that was not the case! If you read further in the passage found in Psalms 139, it says

How does passage in how think of

> "I praise you, for I am fearfully and wonderfully made. Wonderful are your works, my soul knows it very well. My frame was not hidden from you, when I was being made in secret, intricately woven in the depths of the earth. Your eyes saw my unformed substance; in your book were written, every one of them, the days that were formed for me, when as yet there was none of them." (Psalm 139:14-16)

that inform us we should

ourselves? Well for one, it should tell us that what God makes, what he fashions in his hands, is wonderful, period. We should know this in our hearts *very well*. When he created us, he was not flying blind either. He saw what he made, just like when he created Adam and Eve, and he saw WE were good. Before we were even formed God saw us, and he sees us now. No one can take those truths from us. Not the guy who does not like us the way we like him, the guy who pretended only to use us, or the guy who just flat-out treats us badly. We need to require respect from our male counterparts, because if we do not, whether we consciously believe so or not, it shows we do not respect ourselves.

Day 5

Showing Respect

The Bible says that we are to love our neighbor's as ourselves (Matthew 19:19). Please do not let anyone treat you with any less respect and consideration than you know you ought to treat them with. But do not treat anyone with any less respect than you think you deserve either. I have seen many examples of young women who do not respect others. Some examples are through their speech and the way they interact with one another, through putting each other down. Also through their actions. And these behaviors and are not exclusively held for the female they interact with, but also occur in male-female interactions. The old saying is true: You must give respect to get respect. But as I stated before, respect must come first from consciously respecting yourself first. If you respect yourself, you will not act in a manner that does not misrepresent who you are as a follower of Christ, and as a single Christian lady. Until God sends us the earthly man that is for us, we must conduct ourselves with self-respect, seeking to honor and glorify God with everything that we do!

How NOT to Get Respect

I cannot do a day about respect, without addressing one of the biggest issues that young women in my season of life deal with in the social arena, namely, fashion. In a society that is so media-driven and self-centered it is harder for young women not to stumble. The media puts intense pressure on young women to look and dress a certain way, which is immodest. The Bible clearly speaks on how women should dress in 1 Timothy 2:9, saying:

"likewise also that women should adorn themselves in respectable apparel, with modesty and self-control, not

God does not want us to call attention to ourselves through the way we dress, wearing revealing clothing that tempts our brothers in Christ. You may get attention, but you will not get R-E-S-P-E-C-T!

Day 6

My Relationship Status

In conclusion, a lot of single Christian ladies have dreamt of the day when their status no longer is "Single". But how many dream of the day when their relationship status with the Lord says "Married"? I have a surprise for you-it already does!! Isaiah 62 likens our relationship with God with that of a bridegroom and a bride, saying in verses 4 and 5 (in sidebar).

We single Christian ladies are not forlorn, kicked to the curb, left out in the cold, or undesirable! We are brides of the Lord who Reigns on High! This status change is a direct result of us accepting Jesus Christ as our personal savior, and believing in our hearts that he died on the cross for our sins. We didn't have to position ourselves in the right pew for us to be seen by God on Sunday; we didn't have to get involved in a ton of ministries so that we be worthy of his attention. God rejoices over us and loves us as is - broken and damaged, hurting and FEELING lonely. Yet if we really thought about it, we are never alone. Our heavenly bridegroom is always with us. Late at night, early in the morning, in the middle of the day HE IS THERE! We can tell him anything, lean on him during any trial.

Isaiah 2:4-5

[4] You shall no more be termed Forsaken, and your land shall no more be termed Desolate, but you shall be called My Delight Is in Her, and your land Married; for the LORD delights in you, and your land shall be married... [5]and as the bridegroom rejoices over the bride, so shall your God

Until we are being led in a relationship or marriage by one of our earthly brothers in Christ, we need to remember our relationship with the Heavenly Bridegroom himself.

Day 7

Having Faith When You Are Undergoing Suffering

Many of us are going through trials that can sometimes seem unbearable and God's Word speaks to us about undergoing suffering in our lives. Or maybe they always feel as though they are unbearable, and we are just waiting for the end. Let me tell you right now, THAT is not how God wants us to live. He wants us to cherish each day that he has given us, and find contentment in our circumstances until he brings us out of them, or until he does call us home. But how do we do that? We do not *feel* like getting out of bed. We do not feel like going to the physical therapist after that horrible accident – we just will never walk again, and that is a fact. In Romans and in 1 Corinthians it talks about how to deal with and think about suffering.

Romans 5:2-5:

> ²Through him we have also obtained access by faith into this grace in which we stand, and we rejoice in hope of the glory of God. ³More than that, we rejoice in our sufferings, knowing that suffering produces endurance, ⁴and endurance produces character, and character produces hope, ⁵and hope does not put us to shame, because God's love has been poured into our hearts through the Holy Spirit who has been given to us.

1 Corinthians 1:3-6:

[3] Blessed be the God and Father of our Lord Jesus Christ, the Father of mercies and God of all comfort,[4] who comforts us in all our affliction, so that we may be able to comfort those who are in any affliction, with the comfort with which we ourselves are comforted by God. [5]For as we share abundantly in Christ's sufferings, so through Christ we share abundantly in comfort too. [6] If we are afflicted, it is for your comfort and salvation; and if we are comforted, it is for your comfort, which you experience when you patiently endure the same sufferings that we suffer.

When Undergoing Trials, Put His Super on Your Natural

One day I was speaking to a good friend of mine who shared something with me that was very important to me and changed how I thought about "waiting on God," not just because of the topic of being single but waiting on God to move in many areas of my life. What they shared with me is the verse in Philippians 4, verse 13, which states "I can do all things through Christ who strengthens me." Per my friend, contrary to the popular belief that this means that God is always going to come through if I just pray to Him, or this situation IS going to change eventually if I just lean on Him, sometimes it won't change. Sometimes what I want to happen will not happen. It will not have anything to do with how much I prayed, how much I cried, or how many devotions I had that week. This is not because God does not love me anymore, or because he is not a just God. On the contrary, it only illuminates how just God is, depending on how you think about it. Think about it this way – because of our sin, we deserve a penalty of death. But instead of death, we get a relationship with our Creator because he sent his ONLY SON to die for our sins. Not any sin that he committed. So, when I look at the fact that I did not get the internship I wanted, or I didn't get the promotion I wanted, or I'm not done with school yet – these are very minor things when you compare them to the grace that God has shown to us. We deserve to die, but instead we are given the opportunity to live eternally with God. All we need to do is follow him.

This is where the super on our natural part comes in. (I bet you were wondering about that!) On our own, we cannot follow God. Our hearts are "deceitful above all things and desperately sick; who can understand (them)?" That is what it says in Jeremiah

17:9. Psalm 139:16 says, "Your eyes saw my unformed substance; in your book were written, every one of them, the days that were formed for me, when as yet there were none of them." God knows what will happen in our lives, and how it will happen. We may not get married; we may not get that promotion. But one thing we will encounter is contentment with following God if we pursue that. Not to say that it will not be difficult and even scary at times but God promised never to leave nor to forsake us. As long as we are seeking him, he will direct and make straight our paths, and put his SUPER on our natural. Sometimes, however, there may be a communication issue between us and God. Read on to find out more about this communication problem.

Can You Hear Me Now?

Everyone these days has a cell phone, right? And not just any cell phone, but an iPhone, or an Android, or a Google phone. We are always texting, emailing, and communicating 24/7 on our devices. But sometimes, there is some interference. Whether we are in a bad area, or their phone is off, or our battery is dying, sometimes it seems impossible to get ahold of people. Isn't it a blessing that we do not have to worry about bad reception when we need to have a little talk with Jesus?

But do we always feel this way? Sometimes there is a little interference going on, but it is not on His end - it is in our hearts. We do not always believe God can hear us, even though he tells us in His Word that he can. 1 John 5:13-15 says this about God hearing us when we come to Him with requests:

> [13] I write these things to you who believe in the name of the Son of God so that you may know that you have eternal life. [14] This is the confidence we have in approaching God: that if we ask anything according to his will, he hears us. [15] And if we know that he hears us—whatever we ask—we know that we have what we asked of him.

It may seem as though what you ask for will never come, never get there, you will never see a way out. You may not, but through prayer God will give you the sense of *peace* and *contentment* to get through the trial. You can find joy in any situation, if you look back to the cross and realize that the penalty for your sins is *death*. Then remember that Jesus Christ died on the cross for your sins, and so that you might have a relationship with the Father. This is the Ultimate Sacrifice, for the Ultimate Gift.

Remember to give praise to God for the gift He has given, and to never let what you

heart is telling you, which is deceitful above all things (Jeremiah 17:9), if it is saying

that you cannot cry out to God.

Bring in the Troops!

You will sometimes experience negative feelings about your walk with God. Whether you are feeling that it is hard to walk the narrow path or you are looking around you and seeing how easy it is for some people to choose the wider one, these things will trouble you. This is the time when you need to bring in reinforcements. In an army, depending on its size, ammunition levels, and the size of the area it is trying to protect, it might be difficult to overcome enemies and obstacles. But you have reinforcements when you are trying to overcome the enemy and obstacles in your life that never tire, never empty, and never give out. Those reinforcements are the Word of God, and the power of prayer. The Word of God is a lifeline, when you are wounded in the battle of life. It will nurse the injuries your heart takes; reading it will give you living water when you feel parched due to lack of being fed by the Spirit when you have not been reading or praying in a while. The Bible will heal your wounds and scars from past relationships that lead to mistrust and hatred. It will refresh you when you read passages like Psalms 23 and let you know that you have reinforcements so you can continue to fight the good fight. Prayer is another lifeline. As the saying goes, prayer changes things. Amid a battle, if it is God's will, God can heal. Or he can bring final peace. He will bring judgment against your enemies, as it says in Psalm 7:6 - Arise, O LORD, in your anger; lift yourself up against the fury of my enemies; awake for me; you have appointed a judgment. Just as the writer of this Psalm called upon the Lord, so can we revolt against our enemies and change the situation. For as it says in Psalm 23 - [4]Even though I walk through the valley of the shadow of death, I will fear no evil, for you are with me; your rod and your staff, they comfort me.

The weapons of the Lord, his rod and staff, will comfort us during battle, even when we are "walking through the valley of the shadow of death." That is a big deal! Even when we are facing death, Jesus is with us! Amen!

Day 11

Listen

Listen to your heart. Listen - I am alone at a crossroads! Hey why can't you listen?!

These are all lyrics from different songs with the word listen in them. Each person is

going through trial or test or at some decision-making point. Who are they listening to?

Who will you listen to when you are tested with being in a relationship with someone

who is not a Christian? Or when you are at a crossroads in your life and there is a left, a

right, and no middle and you must decide what road to take? Who will you listen to

when you in a deep dark depression because you have lost your job (ladies, we get laid

off too!), or your rent is due and you cannot afford to pay and you are about to be

homeless? Who will you listen to?

You should read Psalm 37:25-28 and what is says about what God says to His children

when they are experiencing trial and hardship:

> 25I have been young, and now am old, yet I have not seen the righteous
> forsaken or his children begging for bread.
> 26He is ever lending generously, and his children become a blessing. 27
> Turn away from evil and do good; so shall you dwell forever. 28For the
> LORD loves justice; he will not forsake his saints.

The Book of Psalms is full of examples of God's answer to those who are crying out

because they are in pain, as well as how God takes care of those and who reach out to

Him. Psalm 23 is a great example.   Another great example is Psalm 57:1-4:

Word says will care of when

> 1 Be merciful to me, O God, be merciful to me,
>
> for in you my soul takes refuge;
>
> in the shadow of your wings I will take refuge,
>
> till the storms of destruction pass by.
>
> 2 I cry out to God Most High,
>
> to God who fulfills his purpose for me.
>
> 3 He will send from heaven and save me;
>
> he will put to shame him who tramples on me.
>
> Selah
>
> God will send out his steadfast love and his faithfulness!

listens. you to His when it that He take you, you are

looking at the past due notice? Will you listen when you're faced with a decision that could be life-altering? Will you listen when you are in such a funk that you do not feel like that you have anything left? God loves you, He is listening and He wants you to hear the message that He sent His only begotten son, that whoever believes in Him will not perish, but will have eternal life. This life will be difficult. Jesus lived what has happened in our lives and worse. But Jesus did it living a perfect sinless life. That is what we should strive for. We should strive to listen to the Holy Spirit, His gift to us to remind us that He loves us, He wants to guide us, and that He will never leave us nor forsake us.

Day 12

The Only One You'll Ever Need

All girls dream of being at the altar in a shining white dress, facing their true love. They dream of happily ever after, and spending an eternity with that special person. What would you say if I told you that dream is already a reality and that you have already been arrayed in the most beautiful dress, and the groom of your dreams has already met you down front? Who is this groom you may ask? Well, if you have accepted Jesus Christ as your Savior and Lord, and believe that he died on the cross for your sins, then you are the bride of Christ. The Bible describes you, as a member of His Church, as the Bride of Christ and relates your relationship to Christ with a wife's relationship to her husband, in Ephesians 5 in verses 25-27.

[24]Now as the church submits to Christ, so also wives should submit in everything to their husbands. [25]Husbands, love your wives, as Christ loved the church and gave himself up for her,[26] that he might sanctify her, having cleansed her by the washing of water with the word [27]so that he might present the church to himself in splendor, without spot or wrinkle or any such thing, that she might be holy and without blemish.

Verses twenty-six and twenty-seven describe our Christ's relationship with us, His Church, His bride. The Bible gives tons of examples of how Christ feels about us, and if Christ is our "Heavenly Husband," how are we to treat Him? Ephesians 5:24 says we are to submit to Him like husbands submit to wives. But on a more practical level, we are supposed to love Christ, talk to Him. Build a relationship with Him. Lean on Him. You should be doing all the things wives do with their husbands. Spend time with Him. Get to know Him, through His Word. He's the only one you will truly ever need, and any earthly husband is a gift, which will come with challenges and trials which you Heavenly Husband will never put you through. Because unlike your earthly husband, Christ is perfect, He will never leave you nor forsake you. He is always with you. He's the Only One You'll Ever Need.

Day 13

I Dare You to Let Me Be

God is daring you to let Him be your One and Only. Until God calls you to married life, he is the only one worthy of being held in your arms. Some of us may have heard that song by Adele, entitled One and Only from her album, 21. It's a beautiful song. But put it in a godly perspective for a second. Think

of the first verse and the chorus as a conversation between you and God

---

God: You've been on my mind, I grow fonder every day, lose myself in time just thinking of your face.

You: God only knows why it's taken me so long to let my doubts go.

 You're the only one that I want.

I don't know why I'm scared, I've been here before, each and every word, I've imagined it all.

God: You'll never know if you never try, to forgive your past and simply be mine!

God loves you. It is all over His Word. In the fact that he sent his Son to die for you, to establish a relationship with you, to draw you close to Him. He wants to spend time with you and to love on you and to shower you with gifts and affection. But he cannot do that if you guys have a long-distance relationship, as in when you pray you act like you are on a long-distance call and just get out the essentials, bring him up to date in as concise a way as possible, then hang up to maybe talk again in a month or two. God wants a daily, personal relationship. He has written one giant love letter to you called the Bible. If you do not read it, you will never find out how much He cares about you or what He has done for you. You will never truly know His love. A world without knowing God's love - What a sad reality to live in!

Day 14

Luv U Back

When God says, he loves us, he does it in huge ways. He provides for us. He protects us. He blesses and takes care of us when we need it. Matthew Chapter 5 verses 3-12 talk about this:

Blessed are the poor in spirit, for theirs is the kingdom of heaven.

Blessed are those who mourn, for they shall be comforted.

Blessed are the meek, for they shall inherit the earth.

Blessed are those who hunger and thirst for righteousness, for they shall be satisfied.

Blessed are the merciful, for they shall receive mercy.

Blessed are the pure in heart, for they shall see God.

Blessed are the peacemakers, for they shall be called sons of God.

Blessed are those who are persecuted for righteousness' sake, for theirs is the kingdom of heaven.

Blessed are you when others revile you and persecute you and utter all kinds of evil against you falsely on my account.

Rejoice and be glad, for your reward is great in heaven, for so they persecuted the prophets who were before you.

His promises to us are many. He treats us and cherishes us because we are His children. Like children, however, we do not always show God the appreciation He deserves. It's almost as if He has left us a very long voicemail, explaining how He loves and cares about us and will never leave us or forsake us as long as we shall live, and we turn around and text Him, Luv U Back. No! We need to show our appreciation to God with more than just a few poorly spelled words in a text message. We need to show God with not just our words, but our actions and lives that we love Him.

Day 15

Who is the Love of Our Lives?

In our minds, we know that God should be our primary focus as single ladies. He should be our all in all, the love of our lives. But more times than not, the Lord is not our primary focus, we do not *feel* like he is our all in all, he is not the love of our lives. We get caught up in different things, and some of them are not necessarily even bad things, like getting good grades for example. It is not bad to want to get a good grade in a class, but when you are spending all your time and energy and neglecting to do what God has called you to do, Houston, we have a problem! He has called you in the time when you are single to draw close to Him, to learn about Him, and to love HIM. He is to be the love of your life. Not Leonardo DiCaprio, or Reggie Bush, or Lebron James. Not the cute guy in your English class, who if you could JUST GET HIM TO NOTICE YOU, you already have your wedding dress and baby names picked out. Ladies, this post is preaching directly to me as it is to you, because I struggle with the same things. We all do. Whether we would like to admit it or not, until we are completely at peace and content with being single, and focused on His work and Him, we are going to wander in the wilderness. It's not going to be pleasant.

Because what we are doing and this might not be a pleasant thing to hear, is we are *worshipping* something other than God when we put all our energies into it and none into God. Our God is a jealous God, and it says so right in Exodus 34:14 which says, "(for you shall worship no other god, for the Lord, whose name is Jealous, is a jealous God). He does not accept our excuses that our lives are busy, that we have over-committed, He wants us to seek his face every day and involve Him in every aspect of our lives. Ultimately, He IS involved in every aspect of our lives, whether we choose to acknowledge Him or not.

On the contrary, if we choose to involve God in every area of our life, we will see a change; we will see the blessings. If we make God the love of our lives and draw close to Him, we will experience a relationship that is better than any relationship we will experience here on earth. 1 Corinthians 8:3 says, "But if anyone loves God, he is known by God." God is the ultimate Creator, our Father, our Savior, he is omnipresent ("everywhere), and he is omniscient (all-knowing). This sounds like the perfect love to me! He is everywhere you need him to be, whenever you need him, and he knows everything you are going through and just wants to hear from you so he can console you and help you through it! Can you think of a time when you were close to God, and leaned on him in a situation? Meditate on that time, and if you like, share it here! It is always encouraging to hear how God works in others' lives!

Day 16

Living in the Light of Eternal Life

So often we get wrapped up in our lives here on Earth. We worry about money, school, work, and relationships. We worry about how we are going to find time to do everything that we have on our lists to accomplish. We look back and regret the fact that we did not accomplish what we had set out to do before the day was over. But have we ever thought that maybe, we did everything that we were supposed to do that day, and that just maybe, there is a bigger goal that we are called to.

Many of us have goals; goals to get a great job, to have a spouse and family. But the result of these goals is only temporal. Children grow up and move away, jobs lay us off, spouses die. But one thing is eternal, and that is our relationship with Jesus Christ. John 12:25 speaks on loving this life on Earth more than we are anticipating and looking forward to living eternally in heaven:

Whoever loves his life loses it, and whoever hates his life in this world will keep it for eternal life.

So, while we should not totally abandon common sense and forget about taking care of our earthly bodies, we still should not get swept away like a broken mast into the sea of the world's whirlpool. We should be more concerned about how to please our Father in our day to day lives than how to please our earthly desires.

God loves you and wants to have a relationship with you! Stay blessed and seek first the kingdom!

The Treadmill of Temptation

They say temptation can be for us like an electric socket for a child: curious, desirable, and something new that we may not have experienced before. The pull can be so strong, that on our own we would not be able to resist. But combined with fear of punishment or consequences, and maybe some experience under a child's belt, the temptation can become easier and easier to overcome. It's like that for us as Christians, although we have an added incentive to resisting temptation: pleasing the Lord.

The path to resisting temptation is a daily one, and can be likened to the time spent on a treadmill to someone who is just starting out. At first, level 1 is difficult. Level one 1 on a treadmill is likened to the days when you are a new Christian. The challenges may feel overwhelming, because you are just beginning to learn to rely on and trust in God. Then you progress to level 2, where those same temptations at level 1 are not as much of a challenge, but you begin to become more aware of other areas that are challenging that you need to fight; you start to grow in the knowledge of what it takes to be a follower of Christ. The treadmill is starting to go faster, you are getting on it for longer, and there are good days and bad days. But finally, you feel like you can handle level 3. So, you wake up one morning determined to give it a try: and you fall off the treadmill! You literally fall, and not only do you fall, but you injure your leg! And you have been bragging to your girl friends about your weight loss progress! You are humiliated, you feel condemned about your behavior, and you are unwilling to tell anybody about the injury.

If anyone asks about your weight loss program, you make excuses. This is how sin can be in our lives: Leaning on our own strength, we will eventually fail to achieve perfection and righteousness, because we are imperfect. It does not matter how well it *seems* like we are doing, or how far we have come since our last win or loss against temptation. And if we are leaning on our own strength, and we fall, there is a huge temptation to keep it in the dark. Romans 3:10-12 says this:

> [10]as it is written: "None is righteous, no, not one;
>
> [11]no one understands; no one seeks for God.
>
> [12]All have turned aside; together they have become worthless;
>
> no one does good, not even one."

On our own NO ONE can resist temptation, and no one should have to fight all temptation alone. Reach out to God and to others my fellow single ladies, and know that you are not alone in fighting the temptations, for there is "No temptation has overtaken you that is not common to man. God is faithful, and he will not let you be tempted beyond your ability, but with the temptation he will also provide the way of escape, that you may be able to endure it." (1Corinthians 10:13)

Day 18

The Cool People Seat

We will never get away from feeling like we want to be a part of the "in-crowd." From the playground of kindergarten, to the cafeteria of high school, to the break room at work. We want to feel accepted, appreciated, loved. These are not in and of themselves bad feelings. But they are just feelings, and they can lead to sinful behavior. Not just major sin issues, but even small things like making fun of people. The Bible speaks clearly on that in Psalms 1:1 –" Blessed is the one who does not walk in step with the wicked or stand in the way that sinners take or sit in the company of mockers". God says that we should not associate ourselves with the wicked. Our sinful nature wants to be accepted by those in the world, but as I stated in the last post, Letter to a Lonely Lady, God says in James 4:4, "You adulterous people! Do you not know that friendship with the world is enmity with God? Therefore, whoever is a friend of the world makes himself an enemy of God."

But what is the alternative? Be outcasts? No! Do not consider yourself an outcast, because you have a new family – a family of people united by their common belief in God. Yes, you will feel lonely sometimes because you may be the target of those sitting in the "Cool People Seat," but remember Jesus was mocked by them during his time.

John 17:14 says, "I have given them your word, and the world has hated them because they are not of the world, just as I am not of the world." He is talking about his followers, and as his modern-day followers, we will experience the same thing. But

Jesus encourages us in Matthew 5 in verses 11-12 – "Blessed are you when others revile you and persecute you and utter all kinds of evil against you falsely on my account. Rejoice and be glad, for your reward is great in heaven, for so they persecuted the prophets who were before you."

Remember when you are feeling lonely, you are not alone. You should reach out to others in the local church who can encourage you in your walk. That is what fellow believers are there for – 1 Corinthians 12:24-26 says "[24] which our more presentable parts do not require. But God has so composed the body, giving greater honor to the part that lacked it, [25]that there may be no division in the body, but that the members may have the same care for one another. [26]If one member suffers, all suffer together; if one member is honored, all rejoice together." God meant for everyone to bear one another's burdens (Galatians 6:2). If you are a lonely lady, lean on your friends in your church community! Also, lean on your Lord and Savior Jesus Christ. Pray and strengthen your relationship with Him, and with these two forces working against your loneliness, you will be alright!

The Temptation to Stay

God loves you. More than anyone ever will. More than any man ever will. If you are in a relationship, and you know deep down the only reason you are in the relationship because you feel lonely, I am speaking to you. Most likely, the person you are with is not the person God would have you be with. Because when you are extremely lonely oftentimes attention from guys, even guys you would not normally allow to pay you attention, looks enticing.

Enticing as it may be, it is dangerous and sinful for you as a Christian to be in a relationship where you are unequally yoked. 2 Corinthians 6:14 says, "Do not be unequally yoked with unbelievers. For what partnership has righteousness with lawlessness? Or what fellowship has light with darkness?" These guys you are entangled with will eventually pressure you to do things that are against your beliefs, because they do not hold to the same standards that you do. They do not have the same moral code. Their lives are lawless in the eyes of God, no matter what religion they claim to hold to, because they do not hold to the law of God. Their eyes have not been opened, and are therefore in the dark.

God calls you to a higher standard than those living in the world. But remember, God will provide for you. Psalm 37:3-5 says, "³ Trust in the LORD, and do good; dwell in the land and befriend faithfulness. ⁴ Delight yourself in the LORD, and he will give you the desires of your heart. ⁵ Commit your way to the LORD; trust in him, and he will act." That is so important to realize. God knows your heart. But he also wants you to delight yourself in Him. Hold onto this. Live your life in such a way that it reminds you of the fact that God loves you, that he desires for you to be happy, and that he will provide for you. But he wants you to make Him the ultimate desire of your heart, not a man. It will only be then when your void of loneliness will be filled. It will be filled with the love of God.

Day 20

The Temptation to Not Forgive Oneself

I am going to talk now about something that I and I am sure many if not all of you have dealt with. Feeling as though you are not saved, or that God cannot forgive you for your sins. Feeling like you can't talk to God because of something you have done. You get a guilty feeling, a condemned feeling, and a sinking feeling that makes you turn inward. It makes you retreat from the light into darkness. And not just any light – you feel like retreating from God's light. Because you feel as though God's light just illuminates your sin. And not only do you feel far away from God, you feel far away from other believers too. You don't want to talk to your other single Christian friends, because you feel ashamed. You feel like they could never have made the mistake that you did. But trust me. Everyone makes mistakes. You would be surprised what another person's story tells, and everyone goes through the temptation to wallow in condemnation.

Romans talks about feeling condemnation because of sin. Romans 8:1-2 says this:

> [1] Therefore, there is now no condemnation for those who are in Christ Jesus, [2] because through Christ Jesus the law of the Spirit who gives life has set you free from the law of sin and death.

Because Jesus Christ died on the cross for our sins we are no longer condemned to death for our sins. We can come to God directly and repent for our sins. We can talk to Him and ask Him for strength to deal with temptation. He loves us.

Jesus Christ died on the cross for us ladies. He died on the cross for sinners. The first chapter of 1st Timothy explains this explicitly:

The

> [12]I thank him who has given me strength, Christ Jesus our Lord, because he judged me faithful, appointing me to his service, [13]though formerly I was a blasphemer, persecutor, and insolent opponent. But I received mercy because I had acted ignorantly in unbelief, [14]and the grace of our Lord overflowed for me with the faith and love that are in Christ Jesus. [15]The saying is trustworthy and deserving of full acceptance, that Christ Jesus came into the world to save sinners, of whom I am the foremost.

author of 1st Timothy is just like us. Before we became saved we were blasphemers, persecutors, insolent opponents to the Word and to God. But because Jesus died on the cross for our sins, and because God opened our eyes, we are opponents of God no longer. Instead we are His. So, when we sin, we can come to Him. He wants us to come to Him. Because HE loved us, He sent His Son so that we could come to Him.

The Temptation to Doubt Our Beauty

We are fearfully and wonderfully made ladies!! Many times, women, me included, have heard from others or just believe within ourselves that the reason why we are not in a relationship has something to do with us physically-we're not enough, thin enough, shapely enough. Put some meat on those bones girl! Then you can attract a man! Or the opposite- You need to slim down!! But is that really the issue? I think not.

God created different shapes and sizes in human beings.

God created us and we are fearfully and wonderfully made. The Psalmist in Psalms 139 knows this and   writes,

> [14]I praise you, for I am fearfully and wonderfully made. Wonderful are your works; my soul knows it very well.
> [15] My frame was not hidden from you when I was being made in secret,
> intricately woven in the depths of the earth.

Two things about these verses stick out to me. The Psalmist knows that what God creates is WONDERFUL. The Psalmist also states that his frame was not hidden from the Lord when he was being made. So, God was not flying blind when he created you. He didn't close his eyes and pull some body parts out of a cookie jar to create you, then place the finished product, unseen by His own eyes, in your mother's womb. No! He saw you, he saw what he created was WONDERFUL, and he was pleased with you. Just the way you are.

Now if you are unhealthily underweight to the point where it is a health concern that is something else. The Bible says this in 1 Corinthians 6:19-20,

[19]Or do you not know that your body is a temple of the Holy Spirit within you, whom you have from God? You are not your own, [20] for you were bought with a price. So, glorify God in your body.

The Bible also says don't let your weight get so out of hand that your health is at risk. Because your body is a temple that is not your own as the verse says, housing the Holy Spirit. And if food is an idol in your life, then your weight will reflect that. Instead, your body should reflect temperance, which glorifies God. So, the temptation to not care and just let go is there as well.

The most important thing is that we are fearfully and wonderfully made, God made us good, just the way we are. The temptation is to doubt that we are beautiful often stems from not understanding where true beauty lies. 1 Peter 3:3-4 tell us a little about God's expectations:

> Do not let your adorning be external—the braiding of hair and the putting on of gold jewelry, or the clothing you wear— but let your adorning be the hidden person of the heart with the imperishable beauty of a gentle and quiet spirit, which in God's sight is very precious.

Day 21

Rock. R&B. Hip-Hop. Pop.

What do these things have in common? They all would be described as secular music.

Many people would say they would not listen to them, even if it was, Christian rock,

contemporary gospel, gospel hip-hop, and contemporary Christian music. Some people

only listen to very traditional music, and say that *that* is the only kind of music that

glorifies God and that we should be listening to. Depending on the person, their

maturity in their walk with the Lord, and the level that this is a temptation for them, to a

certain extent I would agree. Allow me to explain.

Most songs these days talk about love – unrequited love, broken hearts, people in love,

that sort of thing. Rarely do you hear a song about brotherly love or agape love. Can

you think of any popular ones right now? Hearing about people who are drowning in

bad relationships, or drowning because they just got out of bad ones, is not healthy.

Especially if this is all you hear. You will start to grow discontent with your state of

singlehood, because you have not heard any positive messages about it. All you hear are

messages that are either glorifying relationships, or trashing them. Although the music

might provide a sense of entertainment or enjoyment to you, if it is causing you to

stumble, you should let it go, at least until you grow some more. Matthew 5:30 says this

about temptations such as these, "And if your right hand causes you to stumble, cut it off

and throw it away. It is better for you to lose one part of your body than for your whole body to go into hell." The temptation to be in a relationship might become stronger for you if you are constantly listening to that type of music without a buffer, until it is hard for you, without God, to resist giving into some sort of sin. That is why we must, as single ladies, be ever vigilant and guard our hearts and minds.

Dear Lonely Lady

We all feel lonely sometimes on our Christian walk...who am I kidding? We will feel

lonely a lot! We will feel alone, persecuted, and judged - like the world is against us.

But we should not seek out the world to fill the void of loneliness. The Bible states

how we should feel about the world - James 4:4, "You adulterous people! Do you not

know that friendship with the world is enmity with God? Therefore, whoever wishes to

be a friend of the world makes himself an enemy of God." It might feel at times that

friendship with the world is easier, especially as a new Christian who is used to living in

the world, but we need to live considering eternity and because we have a relationship

with God. In addition, we need to remember that we have the local church, God's body

of believers, to fellowship with, cry with, lean on, and laugh with. We as sisters need to

band together and lean on one another.

But our relationship with God will trump everything. God will be there when we are at

our lowest point. We can cry out to Him at any time.

[14] "You are the light of the world. A city set on a hill cannot be hidden. [15] Nor do people

light a lamp and put it under a basket, but on a stand, and it gives light to all in the

house. [16]In the same way, let your light shine before others, so that they may see your

good works and give glory to your Father who is in heaven." Mark 5:14-16

Ladies, we as young Christian women are called to be lights. Our world is a dark one. The people who live in it have clouded hearts. A lot of times we feel as though we should shrink to "fit in," that we can't let our lights and talents shine. We can't be as smart in the classrooms or as savvy in the boardrooms or as witty in the workplace. But is that really glorifying God? He has given every one of us gifts, and to use them in his name is to bring glory to him.

Another cause and effect reaction of being a light is that we may be shunned or outcast in different situations. We may be talked about or slandered; the Bible speaks about this clearly in His Word.

"Blessed are you when others revile you and persecute you and utter all kinds of evil against you falsely on my account." Matthew 5:11

As lights of the world we need to be praying to God that people see Him when they look at us. That they know that we are Christians when we are in these situations such as the workplace or the classroom, and that God is with us and that is the reason why we are successful. Don't succumb to the pressure and the people who tell you that you do not belong in the place that God has for you. Loneliness is a feeling, but God is much greater than our feelings and can give us the peace that surpasses all understanding. Give glory to God for your triumphs and accomplishments, and let your light shine for all to see.

Setting Standards and Sticking to Them

Every girl who wants to be in a relationship, and has ever been in a relationship before has dealt with this issue. Whether it was a good relationship or a bad one, girls set standards and stick to them, or they don't. What I've learned from my mistakes and talking to people more knowledgeable than I, is that there is a voice inside of you, your inner voice let's call it. That inner voice will let you know when a person doesn't meet your standards, and when you should not be with them. And as your walk gets stronger, this voice gets stronger and louder. Another name for this voice is Wisdom. The thing about Wisdom, is she cares about you when no one else is there. When you think you are alone by yourself with no one to call on for advice, I know it sounds corny but, look inside yourself. The voice of Wisdom as mentioned before is inside each one of us, and is an invaluable tool in our Christian walk. Not just because of the aim to set standards and stick to them, but because that voice will lead us in all our decisions. But on the topic of our single life and staying pure in our relationships, listening to the Wisdom of our Spirits and other people is vitally important. The world can be a cruel place, and Wisdom can save us from disaster. Another voice for wisdom is the Holy Spirit. The Holy Spirit is God's gift to us, an internal compass providing wisdom and pointing us in the right direction. Choosing to listen to the Holy Spirit, is choosing the right and blessed path. Even though you may feel lonely, and want a relationship, loneliness being single is nothing compared to the loneliness of being married, yet unequally yoked.

The Devil Wears Armani

The worst men for us ladies can be the most appealing to us. It is the sin nature within all of us that makes these men attractive to us. These men will try and be friends with us, and wear on us, until they have whittled away at our defenses and gotten us in vulnerable positions. Some women are strong enough to just be friends with good-looking or charismatic guys. I know that this is something I struggle with. If you struggle like me, then it is possible that it is a good idea for you, like me, to limit the amount and type of time you spend with your guy friend. Because sooner or later someone is going to start liking someone if you spend a lot of time, for example, talking on the phone together at all hours of the day and night. It's just a reality. And most likely, it's going to be you. I know that has been the case for me. And someone almost always ends up hurt, because the other can't or doesn't want to handle being in that position. There are a few exceptions. But exceptions do not make the rule.

If you know that having a lot of male friends is a temptation for you to lust or to struggle with making an idol out of relationships, the Bible tells you to flee from temptation. Flee means RUN FAST! Not get around to it, eventually. You need to guard your heart in this area and not give temptation any ground. And understand me clearly, this is something that I struggle with. But the difference with me struggling with it now and in the past, is this: I have a Savior who I am leaning on, who has always been there and who I am now calling on to give me strength. Wisdom. Guidance. I used to think to myself, and maybe you do or have done this at one point, that I've got this! I can handle having all these friendships with all these different people. I don't have to be accountable to anyone for what I do. I'm good! But now I know that the verses Proverbs 3:5-7 are true. They state:

> [5] Trust in the LORD with all your heart,
>
> and do not lean on your own understanding.
>
> [6]In all your ways acknowledge him,
>
> and he will make straight your paths.
>
> [7] Be not wise in your own eyes;
>
> fear the LORD, and turn away from evil.

God has been making straight my paths. He has been leading me on a journey and I have been growing so much in my Christian walk as a single Christian lady. Because I know I don't know everything, it frees me to go to my Heavenly Father and learn the right way. It frees me to seek counsel from those I trust and move in the right direction.

The men who come into our lives who are not saved may look good; they may drive fancy cars and wear fancy clothes. Giorgio Armani even. But they are nothing but servants of the devil in Armani clothing if they are not serving the Lord. So, watch out my fellow single Christian ladies. Be on guard and stay prayed up. For if you don't lean on your own understanding about what YOU can handle, but deal in what's wisdom, then God will illuminate your path.

How to Show Grace When You Are Tempted to Not Forgive

Have you ever felt so offended by someone's blatant disregard for your feelings that you feel as though it is just unforgivable? Have you ever written someone off because of what they did to you, not talking to them for weeks, months, or even years? Maybe you still don't talk to them.

Is that of God? Is that loving your neighbor as yourself? Because when we commit a sin against another, we desire to be reconciled with that person. Furthermore, God specifically speaks on forgiving others in Matthew 6:14, which states that "if you forgive others their trespasses, your Heavenly Father will also forgive you." So, there are consequences to not forgiving someone; it does not only affect your relationship with the person, but also your relationship with God. In verse 15 it states," but if you do not forgive others their trespasses, neither will your Father forgive your trespasses." You must consider whether these consequences are worth the pleasure you may feel as you indulge in a lack of forgiveness and harboring bitterness in your heart. Because if we admit it to ourselves, we don't have to admit it to anyone else, we get SOMETHING out of not forgiving a person. Whether it be pleasure at seeing them trying to make it up to us, pleasure in seeing them hurt as much as we did and do, we get something out of it. But is that what we really want? Because that is not all we get. We also get, as stated before, a blind eye turned toward us when it comes to God forgiving us. Many people have memorized verse 14, but 15 is not spoken of as much. However, it is just as important.

So, what does forgiveness look like? Matthew 18:21 says that we are to forgive our neighbor as many as 70 times 7 times. Then in the same passage, Jesus goes on to give the story of the unforgiving servant. In the parable, the servant is forgiven an enormous sum from his master, then turns around and demands a lesser sum from another servant. Then, upon hearing that he cannot pay, he has him thrown in jail. The servant, who had been forgiven his own debt, was then thrown into jail by his master, for not showing forgiveness to his fellow servant. This is how the Lord will be with us if we do not forgive the people in our lives who have hurt us, angered us, embittered us, and wronged us. I am working on this just as you are. But if we, with the help of our Lord and Savior Jesus Christ band together as single ladies, we can overcome unforgiving feelings. We can move past these experiences and people and move on with our lives.

Although we are called to forgive, we do not have to forget. If someone has wronged you repeatedly, do not continue to expect that person to behave differently. Once someone shows you how they are, believe them!

Day 25

The Temptation Not to Listen

Every girl who wants to be in a relationship, and has ever

been in a relationship before has dealt with this issue.

Whether it was a good relationship or a bad one. They both

set standards and stuck to them, or they didn't. I've been in

a few relationships, and I can say that I am not the best at

following this mantra. But what I've learned from my

mistakes and talking to people more knowledgeable than I,

is that there is a voice inside of you, your inner voice let's

call it. That inner voice will let you know when a person

doesn't meet your standards, and when you should not be

with them. And as your walk gets stronger, this voice gets

stronger and louder. Another name for this voice is

Wisdom. I was recently in a situation where Wisdom's

voice was ringing loud in my ear, on this very topic of

relationships, and for a day I ignored her. But the thing

about Wisdom, is she cares about you when no one else is

there. When you think, you are alone by yourself with no one to call on for advice, I know it sounds corny but, look inside yourself. Listen out for the voice of Wisdom. Because the Bible speaks explicitly about the voice of Wisdom, calls her by name, and tells you of the consequences of ignoring her. It talks about this in Proverbs 1. This is a lengthy passage, but it is worth reading the warning. Read the sidebar to take it all in. The voice of Wisdom is inside each one of us, and is an invaluable tool in our Christian walk. Not just because of the aim to set standards and stick to them, but because that voice will lead us in all our decisions. But on the topic of our single life and staying pure in our relationships, listening to the Wisdom of our Spirits and other people is vitally important. Both to our spiritual growth, but really to our health and safety as well. The world can be a cruel place, and Wisdom can save us from disaster.

Proverbs 1:23b-28

I will make my words known to you.
24 Because I have called and you refused to listen, have stretched out my hand and no one has heeded,
25because you have ignored all my counsel and would have none of my reproof,
26I also will laugh at your calamity; I will mock when terror strikes you…anguish come upon you.
28 Then they will call upon me, but I will not answer.

Day 26

Temptation to Shrink When We Are Supposed to Shout the Good News

I do not have to face the knowledge every day that it is illegal in my country to speak the gospel or listen to it preached. I do not face the death penalty for giving a Bible to a non-believer or for even having a quiet time in the Word in my own house. So why is it sometimes hard for me, and for others of you in like situations, to spread the good news about Jesus to others? Is it fear of man? Lack of knowledge? A combination of both? Or some other concern? Now right here, I could say, there are missionaries who put themselves in harm's way every day, some of whom end up having to give their lives because of their decision to spread the gospel to all nations. This would be true. But I think more significantly, and this is not trying to downplay the sacrifices that Christians are making, but still – more importantly, GOD says "Go therefore and make disciples of all nations, baptizing them in the name of the Father and of the Son and of the Holy Spirit…" (Matthew 28:19). God tells us to go out and speak about Him to others, everywhere we go, in all nations, meaning wherever we are. This is a command from God, and that is why it is important. I went to a conference one, and one of the last speakers was R.C. Sproul. One of the quotes that I came away with, that references a license plate and applies to the topic can be summarized to say this: It shouldn't read, "God said it. I believe it. That settles it. Instead it should read, God said it. That settles it." We should not witness just because others are doing it but because witnessing is what God calls us to do. If we do not feel equipped, get equipped, read your Bibles, get books. This is not just for single guys to do ladies; we are ALL called to do God's work

and His will.

How to Save Your Life

Everyone always wants to be prepared for bad situations. If a hurricane comes, people need food and water. If a robber comes, you would like to know how to defend yourself, or at least how to get away unharmed. If an unexpected bill comes, you would want some extra money set aside, enough to cover it. People want to live comfortable lives. But living for Jesus is not always comfortable. There will be times when you will just have to trust him. Most people, if they were given the opportunity, would rather live rich lives of ease than to struggle and just get by, but have the knowledge in their heart that they are going to heaven. Many people can live within their means, but would rather have the fancy cars and the house and the clothes, so they live outside of their means. They do not believe God would not want them to have these things, because they are "good" things, so they sacrifice and scrimp and scrape and throw up a facade like they really can afford these things. They are not living a balanced life, but instead can get caught up in living their daily lives pursuing the things of this world. These people believe the road to a good life is paved in gold, but God says to take up His cross daily and follow Him.

In Luke 9:23-26 it says these words:

> And he said to all, If anyone would come after me, let him deny himself and take up his cross daily and follow me. For whoever would save his life will lose it, but whoever loses his life for my sake will save it. For what does it profit a man if he gains the whole world and loses or forfeits himself? For whoever is ashamed of me and my words, of him will the Son of Man be ashamed when he comes in his glory and the glory of the Father and of the holy angels.

Deny myself? Lose my life? That can sometimes be a hard pill to swallow for anyone. Who wants to deny yourself the things that bring you gratification? No one!! This is because we are merely creatures of the flesh, *who have been saved,* by the blood of Jesus. On our own we cannot save our own lives. If we spend our lives dedicated to trying to accumulate earthly possessions to make our lives *comfortable*, the Bible says we will forfeit the very life we are trying to preserve. We should be living with, not an earthly, but an eternal, perspective. On the other hand, God does not want us to have miserable unfulfilling lives. Matthew 6 tells us not to be anxious about anything, but that God will take care of us, just as he cares for the grass of the field and other things in nature. It says in verse 33, "Seek first the kingdom of God and His righteousness, and all these things will be added to you." Praise God that we have an option, and take advantage of the fact that we have an opportunity to participate in an eternal life with our Heavenly Father.

Day 28

Avoid Them

Before I take a chapter to deal with loneliness head on, I need to deal with one of the root causes of loneliness for single Christian women who either have been in or are in a relationship that is not God-glorifying. As we stated in the previous chapter, the men in these relationships have "looked good." Many of us have either in the past, or in the present, sought after or entertained relationships that were not healthy and not God glorifying, because we were lonely. We run into these relationships with men who don't honor God, don't honor their parents, don't exemplify the fruits of the spirit, and in turn, don't honor us as women of God. 2 Timothy 3 predicts that this will happen. It states this in its first few verses:

But understand this, that in the last days there will come times of difficulty. 2 For people will be lovers of self, lovers of money, proud, arrogant, abusive, disobedient to their parents, ungrateful, unholy, 3 heartless, unappeasable, slanderous, without self-control, brutal, not loving good, 4 treacherous, reckless, swollen with conceit, lovers of pleasure rather than lovers of God, 5 having the appearance of godliness, but denying its power. Avoid such people. 6 For among them are those who creep into households and capture weak women, burdened with sins and led astray by various passions, 7 always learning and never able to arrive at a knowledge of the truth.

Ladies the devil is waiting for you to fall victim to one of his soldiers in his army, so that you may end up "burdened with sins and led astray by various passions, always learning and never able to arrive at a knowledge of the truth." How many times will you receive an 'aha!' moment when someone speaks truth into your life before it sinks in? If any description of a person you have been in an ungodly relationship with or any of the things that have been stated in this section of the book resonate with you, this chapter is for you. Even if it you do not recognize it in your own life yet, this chapter is also for you, so that if you do encounter this later down the line, it will help you to recall this chapter and its Scriptures and words to your memory.

Loneliness: The Real Deal

Loneliness is real. There is no sweeping it under the table, pretending it's not there, tiptoeing around Loneliness the Elephant in the Room. You cannot walk around all your days with a china doll face with a smile painted on, loneliness will manifest itself in some way shape or form, whether it creeps up in your thought life or seeps out in how you carry yourself and your actions. If you do not know how to deal with loneliness, then it can become a real burden instead of pointing you to the One who can fill the void of loneliness in your life. Some people fill their "half-empty" cup with activities, some with busy social lives that are in the end not fulfilling in the long run, others with addictions. Addictions do not have to be just drugs or alcohol either; being a serial dater is a sign of someone who is not okay with just being by themselves. But none of these solutions can fill a heart that is truly longing and lonely. I know from experience, and often get "selective memory" in regards to, the fact that being in a relationship is not the cure to loneliness.

In my experience, I have dated people back to back, without giving much room to breathe and to reflect. I thought that the people I was with would fill the void I was experiencing by not focusing on a relationship with God, but instead, interpersonal relationships with man. That person cannot be there and will not be there 24/7 to fill up your "Loneliness Meter." They are not omnipresent, neither are they capable of providing you with the kind of emotional, spiritual and mental support, no matter whether they would like to or not. That is just reality. So, if that is the real deal, what are some real practical solutions? The first and one of the most important solutions is to as a Christian tend to your relationship with your Lord, Jesus Christ through prayer. With that, we should study the different names of God and their meanings, to remind ourselves of how the meanings of His names relay how He relates to us and what they tell us about his character. Some names to look at here. Here is a list of some that pertain particularly to this, found at https://bible.org/article/names-god.

• Yahweh Jireh (Yireh): "The Lord will provide." Stresses God's provision for His people (Gen. 22:14).

• Yahweh Nissi: "The Lord is my Banner." Stresses that God is our rallying point and our means of victory; the one who fights for His people (Ex. 17:15)

• Yahweh Maccaddeshcem: "The Lord your Sanctifier." Portrays the Lord as our means of sanctification or as the one who sets believers apart for His purposes (Ex. 31:13).

• Yahweh Ro'i: "The Lord my Shepherd." Portrays the Lord as the Shepherd who cares for His people as a shepherd cares for the sheep of his pasture (Ps. 23:1).

Each of these names show how God combats loneliness - He will provide for you, when you are feeling defeated and like no one is in your corner He is your "means of victory," he will fight for you. He set you apart as someone special with a purpose. Finally, he cares for you like a shepherd cares for his sheep.

Red Light, Green Light

Do you remember playing Red Light, Green Light as a child? The ultimate game of patience and at the same time speed, a game that both thrills and chills? It is thrilling to win, but often chilling to face the sting of defeat. When someone says green light, you may get a little closer to them, but as soon as they say red light you must freeze. Do not move. Do not pass go. To you, it seems arbitrary; it is totally out of your hands. But to the moderator, it may not be so arbitrary at all.

Playing red light, green light is a lot like life. Sometimes the light of life is green, and you are moving full steam ahead, stretching out towards a prize. Other times it is red, and you must wait. But in the game of life, the red lights are a lot longer at times, the moderator, God Himself. Nothing He does is arbitrary, and although it might seem like it, He is not trying to tempt you with stops and starts. However, each roadblock in the road to achieving your goals can sometimes be very trying. You will not always be able to go to someone and have them empathize with your situation. You sometimes may have to go it alone, and you will feel like inching forward to get an edge on your issues. But you also know there are consequences for cheating, for not waiting on God's instruction to move. So, you wait; and wait; and wait. A week goes by, then a month, then you feel like you are in a season of waiting and being tempted to go when you know you should stop. God may have someone for you, he may not. A man is not the goal ladies. Peace on Earth, then eternal life in heaven is the goal! Instead of fighting for a man's heart and affections, you need to fight for the peace that surpasses all understanding, letting God be your commanding officer. If you focus on the fact that you are at a red light, and nobody seems to understand where you are at, you will feel lonely. Because you are forgetting the one being that will always understand where you are at. That is because He knew what you were going to go through before you went through it. It's just up to you whether you want to lean on your own understanding, or depend on God.

Day 31

Living in Light of Eternal Life

When you have sinned and you know you have sinned in a major way, you don't feel like confessing it to God, to your friend who keeps you accountable for things – heck you do not even want to think about it yourself. So, you may squash it down into the far recesses of your mind for a time. But it will for sure rear its ugly head again and nag you until you at least go to the Lord and ask for forgiveness. But pride and fear of man may cause you to avoid people who you know will ask you how you are doing spiritually. Or you contemplate not going to church at all. Coming from experience, these can be the worst options from you. I have tried to avoid people who I knew cared about my physical health and spiritual health enough to ask. All I ended up doing was isolating myself, and feeling worse. It just made it that much harder for me to come back. Conversely, it made forgiveness and clarity that much sweeter. In addition, you cannot run from God. Do not run from what you cannot hide from.

What you cannot hide from is God. So, while you are isolating yourself because of your sin, God is right next to you, chilling, just waiting to hear from you. Then He is watching to see your next move. If your next move is to bob and weave before church starts, tuning out during worship and the sermon, and ducking out after service is over, you run the risk of putting yourself in a position to suffer from the self-inflicted wound of loneliness.

The body of Christ was made to carry one another's burdens, and God calls us to confess our sins to one another.

Galatians 6:2 says this about carrying one another's burdens: "2 Bear one another's burdens, and so fulfill the law of Christ."

James 5:16 says this: "Therefore, confess your sins to one another and pray for one another, that you may be healed. The prayer of a righteous person has great power as it is working."

This does not sound like you should run away at all. Instead it commands us to confess our sins to one another and that if someone comes to you needing to confess that you should pray for them. So, do not judge anyone who comes to you with an issue in their life that they are dealing with. Also, pray and really think about who you go to confess your sin and ask them to pray for you, because, as clichéd as it sounds, prayer really does change things. When you run all you are doing is hurting yourself, because you will start to feel alone and as if you are the only one who struggles with your sin and you are not! Loneliness will start to creep in, trust and believe, and you will start judging others believing that they will judge you for the sin that you have not yet confessed! So instead of assuming and judging others, pick someone you know you can trust and go to them. They may even be able to point you to Scripture you can study that speaks to your issue. First however, go to God. He is always there waiting for you.

We get wrapped up in our lives here on Earth. We worry about money, school, work, and relationships. We worry about how we are going to find time to do everything that we have on our lists to accomplish. We look back and regret the fact that we did not accomplish what we had set out to do before the day was over. We see friends moving on, doing different things, and we feel lonely. But have we ever thought that maybe, we did everything that we were supposed to do that day, and that just maybe, there is a

bigger goal that we are called to and a higher purpose for our lives. John 12:25 speaks

on loving this life on Earth more than we are anticipating and looking forward to living

eternally in heaven:

> Whoever loves his life loses it,
> and whoever hates his life in
> this world will keep it for

So, while we should not totally abandon

common sense and forget about taking care of our earthly bodies, we still should not get

swept away like a broken mast into the sea of the world's whirlpool. We should be more

concerned about how to please our Father in our day to day lives than how to please our

earthly desires.

God loves you and wants to have a relationship with you! Seek first the kingdom!